# 100 INSPIRATIONAL QUOTES BY PLATO

QANA BOOKS

OTHER INSPIRATIONAL BOOKS IN THE SERIES:

100 Inspirational Quotes by Mark Twain
100 Inspirational Quotes by Mahatma Gandhi
100 Inspirational Quotes by Oscar Wilde
100 Inspirational Quotes by Friedrich Nietzsche
100 Inspirational Quotes by Confucius
100 Inspirational Quotes by Aristotle
100 Inspirational Quotes by Malcom X
100 Inspirational Quotes by Gautama Buddha
100 Inspirational Quotes by Ali ibn Abi Talib
100 Inspirational Quotes by Winston Churchill
100 Inspirational Quotes by Bertrand Russell



Cover design by Saracen Studios

ISBN: 9798359150095

# PLATO

Plato was a Greek philosopher during the Classical period in Ancient Greece. He founded the Platonist school of thought and the Academy, the first higher learning institution in Europe.

Along with his teacher, Socrates, and his student, Aristotle, he is a central figure in the history of Ancient Greek philosophy and many Western and Middle Eastern philosophies descended from it.

Plato was an innovator of the written dialogue and dialectic forms in philosophy. He raised problems for what later became all the major areas of both theoretical philosophy and practical philosophy.

4

5

Thinking: the talking of the soul with itself

Opinion is the medium between knowledge and ignorance

Love is a serious mental disease

We can easily forgive a child who is afraid of the dark; the real tragedy of life is when men are afraid of the light

The learning and knowledge that we have, is, at the most, but little compared with that of which we are ignorant

Democracy... is a charming form of government, full of variety and disorder; and dispensing a sort of equality to equals and unequals alike

There are two things a person should never be angry at, what they can help, and what they cannot

Honesty is for the most part less profitable than dishonesty

Music is the movement of sound to reach the soul for the education of its virtue

One of the penalties for refusing to participate in politics is that you end up being governed by your inferiors

Good people do not need laws to tell them to act responsibly, while bad people will find a way around the laws

The beginning is the most important
part of the work

Courage is knowing what not to fear

The empty vessel makes the loudest sound

The measure of a man is what he does with power

No one is a friend to his friend who does not love in return

Ignorance, the root and stem of all evil

22

There is no harm in repeating a good thing

Let parents bequeath to their children not riches, but the spirit of reverence

When men speak ill of thee, live so as nobody may believe them

Music is a moral law. It gives soul to the universe, wings to the mind, flight to the imagination, and charm and gaiety to life and to everything

Human behavior flows from three main sources: desire, emotion, and knowledge

We are twice armed if we fight with faith

28

At the touch of love, everyone becomes a poet

29

Attention to health is life's greatest hindrance

If a man neglects education, he walks lame to the end of his life

31

Rhetoric is the art of ruling the minds of men

32

Better a little which is well done,
than a great deal imperfectly

Knowledge without justice ought to be called cunning rather than wisdom

Apply yourself both now and in the next life. Without effort, you cannot be prosperous. Though the land be good, You cannot have an abundant crop without cultivation

To be sure I must; and therefore I may assume that your silence gives consent

The first and greatest victory is to conquer yourself; to be conquered by yourself is of all things most shameful and vile

There are three classes of men: lovers of wisdom, lovers of honor, and lovers of gain

People are like dirt. They can either nourish you and help you grow as a person or they can stunt your growth and make you wilt and die

The greatest wealth is to live content with little

Every heart sings a song, incomplete, until another heart whispers back. Those who wish to sing always find a song. At the touch of a lover, everyone becomes a poet

No man should bring children into the world who is unwilling to persevere to the end in their nature and education

42

Death is not the worst that can happen to men

43

Necessity... the mother of invention

This and no other is the root from which a tyrant springs; when he first appears he is a protector

45

When the mind is thinking it is talking to itself

46

Love is the joy of the good, the wonder of the wise, the amazement of the Gods

47

He who commits injustice is ever made more wretched than he who suffers it

Wonder is the feeling of the philosopher, and philosophy begins in wonder

It is right to give every man his due

50

Poetry is nearer to vital truth than history

The man who makes everything that leads to happiness depends upon himself, and not upon other men, has adopted the very best plan for living happily. This is the man of moderation, the man of manly character and of wisdom

52

He who is of calm and happy nature will hardly feel the pressure of age, but to him who is of an opposite disposition youth and age are equally a burden

How can you prove whether at this moment we are sleeping, and all our thoughts are a dream; or whether we are awake, and talking to one another in the waking state

States are as the men, they grow out of human characters

55

# Man - a being in search of meaning

Entire ignorance is not so terrible or extreme an evil, and is far from being the greatest of all; too much cleverness and too much learning, accompanied with ill bringing-up, are far more fatal

Knowledge which is acquired under compulsion obtains no hold on the mind

Truth is the beginning of every good to the gods, and of every good to man

Philosophy begins in wonder

There must always remain something that is antagonistic to good

61

He who steals a little steals with the same wish as he who steals much, but with less power

62

Nothing in the affairs of men is worthy of great anxiety

All the gold which is under or upon the earth is not enough to give in exchange for virtue

64

Courage is a kind of salvation

As the builders say, the larger stones do not lie well without the lesser

Our object in the construction of the state is the greatest happiness of the whole, and not that of any one class

67

The good is the beautiful

A state arises, as I conceive, out of the needs of mankind; no one is self-sufficing, but all of us have many wants

The most virtuous are those who content themselves with being virtuous without seeking to appear so

I never did anything worth doing by accident, nor did any of my inventions come by accident; they came by work

Excess generally causes reaction, and produces a change in the opposite direction, whether it be in the seasons, or in individuals, or in governments

72

Wisdom alone is the science of other sciences

73

Those who intend on becoming great should love neither themselves nor their own things, but only what is just, whether it happens to be done by themselves or others

74

Cunning... is but the low mimic of wisdom

The god of love lives in a state of need. It is a need. It is an urge. It is a homeostatic imbalance. Like hunger and thirst, it's almost impossible to stamp out

When the tyrant has disposed of foreign enemies by conquest or treaty, and there is nothing more to fear from them, then he is always stirring up some war or other, in order that the people may require a leader

We do not learn; and what we call learning is only a process of recollection

There's a victory, and defeat; the first and best of victories, the lowest and worst of defeats which each man gains or sustains at the hands not of another, but of himself

Any man may easily do harm, but not every man can do good to another

Then not only an old man, but also a drunkard, becomes a second time a child

The wisest have the most authority

No one ever teaches well who wants
to teach, or governs well who wants
to govern

Whatever deceives men seems to produce a magical enchantment

Poets utter great and wise things which they do not themselves understand

85

One man cannot practice many arts
with success

The highest reach of injustice is to be deemed just when you are not

The curse of me and my nation is that we always think things can be bettered by immediate action of some sort, any sort rather than no sort

If particulars are to have meaning, there must be universals

89

Not to help justice in her need would be an impiety

I exhort you also to take part in the great combat, which is the combat of life, and greater than every other earthly conflict

91

No law or ordinance is mightier than understanding

The community which has neither poverty nor riches will always have the noblest principles

93

Virtue is relative to the actions and ages of each of us in all that we do

94

Hardly any human being is capable of pursuing two professions or two arts rightly

No one knows whether death, which people fear to be the greatest evil, may not be the greatest good

96

I have hardly ever known a mathematician who was capable of reasoning

I would fain grow old learning many things

Injustice is censured because the censures are afraid of suffering, and not from any fear which they have of doing injustice

To go to the world below, having a soul which is like a vessel full of injustice, is the last and worst of all the evils

Wealth is well known to be a great comforter

When a Benefit is wrongly conferred, the author of the Benefit may often be said to injure

All things will be produced in superior quantity and quality, and with greater ease, when each man works at a single occupation, in accordance with his natural gifts, and at the right moment, without meddling with anything else

Then not only custom, but also nature affirms that to do is more disgraceful than to suffer injustice, and that justice is equality

Knowledge becomes evil if the aim be not virtuous